LETTERS TO MY TEACHER

LETTERS TO
MY TEACHER

DAGOBERT D. RUNES

THE WISDOM LIBRARY

A Division of
PHILOSOPHICAL LIBRARY
New York

CONTENTS

ROSES UPON THE ROGUES

My dear Teacher:

QUITE a few decades have passed since I left your classroom in that little Austrian university town. Time has traveled at quickstep, with infinite misery stumbling close behind.

You ask me if your lessons of old have stood up under the tests of a new era and a new hemisphere. Yours is not a single query; it involves a flock of questions. Which am I to answer first? I hardly know where to begin. I look at the portrait you sent me and I see a withered, spare old man with a sorrowful face, living in a country that was once an empire and now is not much more than a highlight on the international tourist map.

I saw the Empire yet in flower—and I saw it crumble and fall apart. And, in melancholy analogy, so very many of the pedagogical structures which you erected before my intent eyes shared the fate of the Austrian Empire.

1

When I was a boy you looked mighty tall to me. You were insistent and voluble and set paragraph upon paragraph like bricks of cement. I felt myself traveling on the train of progress and enlightenment toward a not too distant goal of perfection, from a promising present of accomplishment to a jubilant era of tomorrow's civilization.

I take another look at your portrait, and your wistful demeanor betrays that you share my feeling of disappointment. During those few years that we were given to watch history instead of slipping into it, man may have taken a step or two forward, but the Lord only knows how disastrously far back into barbarism man's boots were marching most of the time.

Our generation has massacred 40 million people in that many years. Of these only a minority died in warfare; the others were put to death—men, women and children—in so-called lawful manner by malevolent usurpers of power and with the consent of the citizens.

No one can deny that Hitler, Stalin and Mao, to name just three of the executioners anointed by the Devil himself, were enjoying enthusiastic popularity among their fellow-men; and that at no time did they fail to receive ecstatic approval of their respective genocides.

There are many smaller examples of present-day man's inhumanity to man. Their great number prohibits enumeration. But the sordid deeds are known to all. Be it that opposing gangsters are assassinated in front of television sets in Cuba with the entire city population of Havana cheering every detail of the butchery; be it that an oil-guided satyr of Araby sits on the throne of a realm where every fifth person is a bound slave, kidnaped from the plains of Africa and sold in the market place—for the favor of such dastardly creatures these things are viewed by the leaders of the West with a benevolent smile and by those of the East with brotherly embrace.

The most disturbing element in this sad panorama is the fact that the masses of the world, eagerly as well as gingerly place garlands of roses upon the shoulders of the evildoers.

What is wrong with education that makes 100 million Germans cheer Hitler; or 200 million Russians mummify Stalin so that the next thousand years may behold him; or 600 million Chinese bow daily before Mao's picture; or 400 million Indians hail Nehru's forked tongue? And, finally, what's wrong with education in some segments of our own country where men will invite a manure-sniffing dog to sleep on their cot and women will place an evil-smelling cat on their bed pillow, but none would permit a colored man to live in the same block or eat at the same counter?

There must be something wrong with education, fundamentally wrong. Let us get down to fundamentals.

I greet you,

GOD IS A LONELY BEING

My dear Teacher:

EVERY epoch in human history has its own gods and has its own devils. They keep changing and, of course, they all travel in different disguises. The Devil may journey about in a monk's habit; the messenger of the good Lord in a fancy shako and sash.

There were times when the evildoers of mankind rode straight out of hell, holding in their outstretched right hand an image of the immortal Jew, Jesus, while with their left they upheld Lucifer, Lilith and Beelzebub. Remember the days of Torquemada. More often than is commonly realized, certain concepts in people's minds have become petrified, and only with difficulty can they be dissuaded from clinging to these traditional notions of "benevolent" and "malevolent" movements, issues and organizations.

The devils of today wear a different masquerade from those of yestercentury. The devils of today wear a muddy and unadorned Marshal's uni-

5

form, or a peasant's tunic, covering their heads with a worker's cap and speaking softly with a worker's inflection. But beneath the artful grimace and gesticulation, to the experienced eye are clearly visible Satan's fleshless fingers and horse-hooved left foot.

Mankind's enemy of today travels under the cloak of a weary friend of labor, and he wins the ear and the heart of the fellow travelers not with threats and not with gifts but with a glib tongue.

The tongue and the pen are the swords of the conquerors of today.

Many of our schools have managed to eject an alleged ancient enemy—religion—from the classroom; and at the same time admitted totalitarian propaganda through the thin subterfuge of "progressivism" and "liberalism" as a replacement.

It is true that in certain centuries religious teachings were permeated by hateful allusions, *pro paganos* and, equally, against the heretics. But the religious leaders today, though they are frequently much too silent for my ears, as far as their teachings go, tell the basic truths of Judaic wisdom and humanity; while the propagandists, under the standards of Communism, teach pitiless hatred against the society and the people living under a democratic government.

The enemy of today is not the Church but the Marxist meeting hall—and by throwing the preacher out and bringing Mao in, we have shut the door to the Lord but not the Devil.

God is a lonely being: be it God the Multiverse, the All in One, Creative Nature, the Infinite in Infinite attributes, then He is all-potent; be it God the spirit of rightful thinking in man, man's conscience, the Shekinah of the Hebrews, then God is *Ens Perfectissimum*. But man is lonely too. And man is self-willed and lasting in the all-fleeting *pantarei*.

God needs no man in His perfection, but man needs God, or life becomes a mere drifting amidst the debris of everyday existence. What good is acquainting the pupil with this or the other detail of his surroundings: letting him know a bit about botany and zoology, a bit about geography and history, how to write and how to read, how to look up nature through its simple laws of physics, and even how to measure distances among a thousand huge rocks whirling through space? What good are these bits of information if the pupil receives no guidance as to how to be a better man among a better people—and God is the word we choose to signify the highest and the best in man's relationship to man. In the words of the great teacher, Baruch Spinoza: man's love to God is nothing but man's love to man.

Without such teaching students will grow into adulthood continuing to be enemies of each other, group fighting group and nation fighting nation

7

in battles more sanguine and more destructive as their tools of warfare increase in complication.

I wish there were a better word for man's *summum bonum* than God; that word has become blurred by misuse and abuse. But until such time we have to cling to that one.

Without the humanities science is merely a conglomerate of deadly cold facts; and without God the humanities are merely an assemblage of arid cultural information.

It is God, or the recognition of an everlasting ethical principle, that can give education a face, and give this face the view of a better tomorrow.

Yours,

THE CLASSROOM TOURNAMENT

My dear Teacher:

MY most vivid recollections of the school years are shot through by memories both emotional and ideological of functioning under highly competitive pressure. Hardly ever was I given a task by you or your colleagues that didn't entail constant lookout for my fellow students. Hardly ever did I sail alone on the sea of knowledge. I was forever racing against my comrades in the lane of Zephyr and Hurricane. I was rarely given the joy of gliding with the winds, be they soft or blustery. My ear was cocked for them, but my eyes were on the race, forever fearful that I might be left behind or remain in dunces' row.

I suppose a race is all right for horses or dogs, although I doubt if it improves their usefulness. I doubt even that car racing betters the understanding of motor power. I am rather inclined towards the cynical concept that horse racing is truly a sport of kings, but I thought that those overbearing, parasitic bluebloods had gone out of style and admiration with the American and French Revolutions. As near as I can see today, animal races, be they horse, dog or bull, are staged for the low-minded to jag their dull imaginations into a feeling of thunder, blood and excitement. And as far as car racing is concerned, spectators come just to see the blood; there is nothing else in the arena that isn't visible to their greedy eyes at the average crossroads.

Then why child races? Why race one student against another in an alleged effort to improve their minds?

Sometimes the average classroom reminds me of the old Japanese clubbing tournaments: you put ten people in a closed arena and let them beat their brains out until one of them comes out the winner. He is the class valedictorian.

It may even be true that the winner in this tournament is the man of the greatest prowess, and deserves a crimson laurel of Carete. But is this our intent, to raise an aristocracy of eggheads, and to the devil with the people?

In the little research I have done, I have found the valedictorian of high school as well as college more often than not somewhere near the bottom of true accomplishment a generation later —which confirms an old adage: "a glorious flower in the hothouse will easily wilt before sun and rain and wind."

So many boys and girls have I seen pass their school years in an aura of glamour, bemedaled and behonored. I tried to follow, for my purposes, their trek, and I found so many of them a sorry lot in later life.

They had learned much in their school years, and as they were gifted with certain proficiencies of memory and quick attention, they excelled in the classroom. But much of what they had acquired turned out to be ill-shaped tools that fitted little of the machinery of life. And what they had to unlearn was considerable; they had to loosen their tenseness of eager competition in an endeavor to fit within a society aiming at cooperation.

There were no medals and no honor scrolls, no Dean's list and no teacher's pets—at least not in the sphere of decent society.

I say "decent society" because some of our grown-up society, too much of it, has been corrupted by the constant outpouring from our schools of mentally and emotionally confused, self-centered juveniles. Those who walked into a plant with their school honor roll raised above their heads had to learn quickly that industry and science, the law and the government, manufacture and distribution, agriculture and utilities, were

11

deeply rooted in working together under the rules of cooperation and had little use for egocentric narcissism.

The man in the factory who demonstrated how he could outdo his fellow workers was quickly sobered up by union as well as management. The professional who tried to publicize his personal talents, pretended or real, was subdued by silence.

There are some countries, especially within the Soviet Empire, in which the roughshod rider, the opportunist, and the denouncer, the overtime speculator and the homework show-off, are bemedaled instead of rejected. But such an attitude is only a sharp reminder of the days when there were only kings and slaves, vying for the princely favors.

When I speak of "decent society" I mean a social organization which is based upon a just and fair distribution of its advantages to all, and free access to them for everybody.

In such a society a school that favors the gifted to the detriment of the others is highly immoral.

What would you say to a school in which only the pretty girls and handsome boys would be the recipients of medals and scrolls, and the ugly ones put under a dunce-cap or even publicly expelled?

What would you say to a school where only

the slim girls and boys would receive the good marks, while the others would be marked low or kicked out? What would you say to a school in which only the redheads would be rewarded?

A pupil can as little help being quick on the trigger or having a lasting memory as he or she can help being good of looks, slim of frame or endowed with a shock of reddish hair. This, in my opinion, is the cardinal and cruel mistake perpetrated by an ancient system of education in which the allegedly gifted are rewarded and the less fortunate set back, despised and exposed to public ridicule. No man ever took the trouble of setting down the miseries which the young have to suffer through their school years because of the presence in their midst of those specially endowed by nature, whose endowment, as I mentioned before, most frequently is only of school duration. But that is a long time in the life of a growing child.

Mind you, I am not speaking here of the retarded or the backward, the sick or the crippled. At this moment I am not speaking of those, but rather of the average pupil in the average school.

I suppose there are many who think of a child's misery as kiddish pangs, worries, fears, hopes—but are they different from our own emotions, except in their object? Are they less biting because they are sustained by the young? Are they less fearful because they are caused by alleged well-meaning persons such as teachers, and interpreted by other well-meaning persons such as parents?

I have seen surgeons and other physicians perform minor operations on children, causing them excruciating pain, without using readily available anesthesia because the children had no way of knowing, as the grownups did, that it all could be done painlessly, as it is done to grownups themselves.

No teacher has the right to stigmatize a child as being inferior because its memory is less formidable than that of others. No teacher has the right to mark a child low or lower because its apparatus of comprehension works in a slower manner than that of others. No teacher has the right to point out the child or mark it publicly because its strength of concentration or span of attention operates on a different depth or length.

If anyone objects to my using the term "publicly," may I explain that to the pupil his colleagues and friends in the classroom are his peers, that is, his public, as your colleagues and friends are your public. He has to spend ten or twenty years of his life in the classroom, labeled by public tests and public evaluations an inferior individual.

How would you like being, let's say, a physician if your bag and your car were marked RATHER MEDIOCRE DOCTOR? Or a lawyer if your

14

briefcase were stamped BARELY 60—SLOPPY—A SHYSTER? Or then again, considering also those on the other side of the fence, how would you like being a pharmacist if you had to post over your shop a sign reading in loud, red letters: TERRIFIC CHAP—A GENIUS? Or a housewife who had to walk about the house in an apron inscribed: WONDERFUL COOK—MAGNIFICENT BREEDER?

Under conditions similar to these, unbelievable as it seems, do our youngsters have to spend the first twenty-odd years of their lives. They are marked by their teachers, and consequently by their parents and the parents of their colleagues as to what they really are, at least in the eyes of the masters of pedagogy. Their accomplishments are counted out—usually in uneven numbers—and these numbers are impressed indelibly not only on various papers and documents, but also upon the hearts of those youngsters and upon the cold faces of the so-called "protective adult body" of parents and neighbors, under whose pressure the children carry on.

I don't know by what secret system the teachers come up with their numbers. I don't want to question their validity; that is not at issue. What I would like to question is their purpose, other than the evil result described above.

Don't they know that our greatest men grew out of mediocre school marks, and vice versa?

But even if making a dog race out of school

were to improve the mentality of the children, I would say that the advantage isn't worth the suffering. *It isn't!*

But does competition improve knowledge? I know it has often made for cribbing, for gross deceit; it has made for envy of schoolmates and antagonism towards teachers; it has made for anxiety, insecurity, and even malice against the lucky ones—but it has never improved true understanding. You can pack a basketful of useless, and even some useful, information into a frightened head, but if you make it your business to follow up that child, you will find that most of it. was tossed out posthaste, frequently right after the exam. And the little that remained could have readily been ensured by cooperative teaching instead of oppressive instruction.

Do you remember the dates to memorize in history, for which Jack walked about like a prize bull and Bill hunched like a pariah in the back of the schoolroom? Do you remember the Greek verbs and the chemical formulae which the same Jack could rattle off whenever the teacher's wand touched his forehead, and which poor Bill never could remember in the required quick time, or perhaps any time? Well, I saw both of them the other day. Neither of them had the slightest appreciation of history, Greek or chemistry. Nothing, but nothing, remained. They were so engrossed in memorizing, one in his success, the other in his failure, that the real subject was all but forgotten. If only one of their teachers had had the courage to throw away his marking pen and had sat down with them as an old fellow among young fellows, and told them of the mysteries and workings, the living and the striving of the people of times gone by; how these people really lived—the farmers and the burghers, the scholars and the peasants, and even the adventurers—instead of enumerating the thousand useless ups and downs of foul kings and vicious queens battling each other for gain and glory on the Eurasian soil.

And instead of trying to cram their minds with a Greek vocabulary, which perhaps one in ten thousand would ever come back to after school, had this teacher sat down and read with them the magnificent poetry and philosophy of ancient Greece, they would have acquired a wealth of lasting wisdom and a sense for true beauty, and felt the touch of the magic words of literature.

And had this same teacher refrained from setting them the task of learning by rote a thousand Latin synonyms for plants and fruits, and instead filled the classroom with some growing plants, or, better yet, taken them for a few weeks or months to a farm where they could truly learn the workings of nature, that would have remained with them.

Such cooperative teaching would bear its own

fruits for the rest of their lives, and would never require the humiliating procedure of smearing with a crayon on the back of each child how it rates in the eyes of its prober, and through him, in the community.

I greet you,

PRODIGIES BY THE WAYSIDE

My dear Teacher:

THE history of the prodigy is full of surprises. The reason why so many people still stand in awe of the prodigy is simply because of their ignorance of the wind-up of most, if not all, prodigious matters. Those practicing husbandry have long known that some cattle will grow more rapidly and mature earlier than others. But when their growth is completed, it is just another horse or another cow, according to their respective breed. Cows do not become mountainous just because they matured earlier, and trees don't grow into the heavens just because they made their rise more rapidly in the first few years than others.

Some years ago I made it my business to study the spin-out of a group of widely acclaimed radio "quiz kids." The statistics after twenty-five years showed not one of them to be above average in either study or accomplishment in later life. In fact, two of the boys whose pictures were frequently in local and even national papers were found in low-grade administrative positions. I remember one boy who entered one of our leading universities at the age of twelve with highest honors in mathematics and physics. He is now, after almost thirty years, a senior bookkeeper in a hospital organization.

Even a cursory study of this subject within one's own circle of friends and acquaintances, if objectively carried out, will demonstrate clearly that the prodigy cult is based upon a misunderstanding of the biological phenomenon that some creatures mature earlier than others, which doesn't even imply that those who mature earlier will equal those who mature more slowly.

An analysis of the great scientists of modern times bears out the fact that the percentage of so-called prodigies among them is basically the same as that among the so-called common people. Quite a few of the most outstanding men of modern history, such as Einstein, Edison, Pasteur, Leonardo da Vinci, Voltaire, Copernicus, Newton, were mediocre students and were completely overshadowed in boyhood days by contemporary "prodigies" who fell by the wayside as the years went on.

In our days quite frequently even teachers and psychologists have misunderstood the character of the prodigy. They have troubled even infants to absorb foreign languages and to become as early as possible adept in reading, in writing, and in the juggling of mathematical figures. The only thing which they accomplish by this procedure, in addition to exhausting the child, is to stiffen the pride of the child by the inevitable admiration of ignorant friends and educators, who so often mistake pre-training for genius. What this world needs is not more of these hothouse plants that will wither anyhow at the first breath of fresh air from the open. What this world needs is deep thought about the problem of how to raise good people in a world beset by evil influence.

I greet you,

BENCH-ATHLETES AND BET-ATHLETES

My dear Teacher:

THE other day I stepped into a bar to make a telephone call. While waiting my turn at the booth I couldn't help overhearing bits of a conversation between two elbow-benders watching a wrestling match on the overhanging television set.

"Y'know, I just love sports," said one of the Red Noses. "I could watch sports all night!"

"So do I," said his companion. "I'm quite a sportsman myself. By the way, I haven't seen the afternoon's scores yet. I got a fin on the Dodgers."

Perhaps this snatch of saloon conversation will throw some light on my refusal to run to the games on Saturdays and Sundays.

Athletics are nice for those in the contest. In fact, that is the true meaning of the word "athletics"—to be in a contest, to compete. I suppose it's only natural for an athlete's friends and associates to want to watch the competitors, but I somehow hate to see myself as a bench-athlete or a bet-athlete. And I'm afraid that our great country has developed millions of purely spectator sportsmen and sportswomen whose interests are for the most part centered on the gossip and betting end of the business.

I do not like athletics as business. I do not like athletics as gamble. I do not like athletics as gossip.

People seem to have forgotten that the competitive aspect of bodily exercises is purely incidental: It almost seems—and this applies especially to our schools and colleges—as if the competitive superstructure of sports activities, with all its publicity and hero-worship, gossip and gamble, and buying and selling of performers like race horses, has overshadowed the true function of bodily exercises which were meant to be engaged in by all the participants and not merely by the stable stars.

To some extent our college and club managers have brought to the gymnasium the atmosphere of the circus, with its commercial fanfare and trappings.

In a college of 4,000 students I hate to see two dozen boys or girls on the playing field and the rest on benches participating only as fans and followers.

Perhaps the whole Greek and Roman concept of athletics ought to be re-examined. The Olympics expressed a special type of competitive rivalry among the various city-republics, and I wonder if it is necessary for our age, with its crying need for international unity, to put so extreme an emphasis on purely national accomplishments. The most recent Olympic Games in Finland, Melbourne, and Rome, showed that such athletic contests, instead of bringing about harmony, serve only to deepen disunion and stimulate competitive jealousy.

As for the athletics of the Roman arena, they seem to have served the Caesars by amusing a disgruntled populace. Let us not forget that this Caesarian practice of *panem et circenses*, bread and circuses, betrays the arrogance of Rome's aristocracy toward the people of the world. The motto bespeaks the true character of Roman athletics—a crude but effective device to keep the masses in an amused mood. Amused people are not likely to be dangerous.

I say again, perhaps it is time for us to drop the Greek and Roman concepts of athletics as circus events, to take the dollar and the competitive sting out of the arena, and to let more people play and fewer people gamble, gossip and gripe.

The disappearance of the grunts of the phony wrestlers may empty the saloons, but it may also help to bring back to wholesome life an ancient sport.

Elimination of the circus salaries given to star players may empty the stables of the monied clubs, but it may encourage many hundreds of thousands to play the game in their own fashion, unembarrassed and uninhibited, instead of just covering the bleachers and throwing pop bottles from the aisles.

The return of pigskin heroes to the classroom and to anonymity may deprive some colleges of the only worthwhile faculty of which they can boast, namely, the one managed by their football coach, but it may help to bring back to schools of higher learning the simple thought which was in the minds, I am sure, of their founders—higher learning.

Schools do not make a circus over a boy or a girl if he or she is particularly good in mathematics, in history or in botany. Then why make such a fuss about a boy simply because he can spiral a ball better in passing, or run crisscross on a football field, or make trick feints at extraordinary speed?

There is an almost forgotten tale about King David and the two horse trainers. The King did not know which one to hire for an impending war, so he asked the two men to bring before him six of their best horses. The first trainer, who was named Abu, brought before the King six remarkable animals. One horse could stand on his hind legs for as long as it would take to recite the Commandments. Another horse could stand on his forelegs and jump. A third could dance; a fourth could swim like a fish; a fifth could carry the load of a camel; and the sixth horse could run as fast backwards as it could forwards.

The King watched these performances with astonishment. Then he called for the second trainer, who brought his team of six stallions, each of which looked pretty much like the other—clean, trim and well-groomed. "What can they do?" asked the King.

"Nothing, Sire," said the trainer, "that any other good horse could not do, only they do it well and do it steadily."

"You are my man," said the King, "because I need horses to carry my men into battle and not into a circus tent."

I greet you,

WALKING WITH A CLENCHED FIST

My dear Teacher:

IN all countries of the Western world, and some of the Eastern, the individual lives under two governments. While he spends his mature years under so-called State authority, be it democratic or otherwise, the young person's first decades are more or less subject to school government. It is only natural that the student will carry over his school political attitudes into his mature social life.

The sins of the teacher, as well as the sins of the school, will be discharged in adult years on victim as well as pupil-perpetrator.

If one learns in school to be self-centered, success-greedy, prize-snatching, merit-hogging, one is not likely to become a self-effacing, co-operative member of society.

If one learns in school to be an apple polisher, an errand seeker, an eye catcher, a sleeve brusher, one will have had expert training in sycophancy. If one learns in school to report the cribbing of fellow students while covering up one's own, the lasting lesson has been brought home that snitching is an accepted way of life, stool-pigeoning a duty. The crime of denunciation assumes the shape of a virtue; and there is no sin if you beat the rap.

In schooling where success is noisily crowned Queen of Achievement and covered with the purple of "A" report cards, principals' gold stars and deans' favorite listings, those who get near the crown live in dread of runners-up and in hopeful excitement of getting there ahead of the others—which makes for envy, false pride, and other evil emotions that deface the Lord's image on which man should model his own.

For a principle of morals that could truly serve all humanity bent on betterment, I should like to paraphrase the old Hebrew adage: "Walk in humility and with an outstretched hand."

They don't teach you to walk in humility with an outstretched hand in these schools of ours. Indeed, I would say if it's possible to reverse this maxim, it could well serve as a motto for present-day pedagogy.

I greet you,

LEARNING AND THE COMMON MAN

My dear Teacher:

ONE of the reasons, perhaps the major reason, why education has made so little progress in comparison with other cultural endeavors over the last thousand years is that much of it has been, and is still, aloof from practical, or even intelligent, purpose.

The study, for instance, of botany and zoology, except for a more detailed and unified systematization of nomenclature, still hangs on the rote learning of hundreds of assorted terms germane to plant structure and animal anatomy, physiology and histology. The so-called major problems in biology, heredity and evolution, are passed over rather lightly with pat responses of Darwinian hypotheses which a ten-year-old, if he were made to think instead of recite, could disprove by such primitive processes of reasoning as: if man, "the highest form of present-day existence," could trace his origin to lower species, e.g. mammals, amphibian creatures, protozoa, even a quorum of

31

gases, the question would arise—who created those gases out of which these trillions of trillions of tons of matter evolved? *Ex nihilo nihilum.*

A sixteen-year-old could reduce many of the so-called theorems in Darwinism to weak-legged hypotheses. As it is, sweating his memory cells into temporary absorption of hundreds of *termini technici* adds little to his understanding, and blocks the latter from getting beneath the skin-wisdom of rote learning. The acquisition of modern categorization in biology encourages as little true research as the medieval memorizing of old-fashioned Aristotelian biological categories.

What generally the schools fail to realize is that the status of a particular body of science in a particular era is, educationally speaking, only a means of encouraging scientific thinking in the student, and it is not an aim in itself. The important thing is to examine and comprehend the processes by which science was deepened and widened. The mere memorization of scientific data is of quite secondary significance; undue stress on the memorizing of parts and particles of animal and plant bodies, with their ancient Latin or Greek surnames, will elevate no mind, but burden many.

Let us look at this situation in retrospect and see of what was dished out in school how much was really wheat and how much was chaff that the winds of worldly life blew away.

How many of those you ask in their mature years can remember the hundred odd names attached to the anatomy of the reptile or the structures of the seemingly endless masses of plant life? How many remember the manifold math problems they had to carry through with little or no understanding of broad mathematical principles? How much use did any of them have of the multiple language courses on which they wasted thousands of hours of their time, instead of reading in easily available, splendid translations the literature of these foreign countries? Some quote the 18th-Century adage: "A gentleman is one who has learned and forgotten his Latin and French." I think this is too heavy a price to pay for being a gentleman.

At this time I should also like to mention again the absurdity of our history teaching, concentrating on rote learning of the lives and loves of the great European kings and conquerors; the miserable manner in which they carried on a blood-spattered existence, made possible only by Church-upheld laws of heredity which allegedly applied to these yellow-hearted princelings of blue blood.

Of what little merit this kind of historic battle report and court gossip is can be deduced from the fact that we in the Western world study not and know not, school-wise, the corresponding history of India, China or Siam while by the same token their peoples know not ours. And they get along fine without it, just as we do.

We would get along much better with our own people, and with others, if we would re-interpret history as the knowledge of the people's events, and not their usurpers' and black knights'; and relegate the study of military and kingly tyrants, bastard or legitimate, to the criminal records for those to examine who have reason or desire to search in the black books of the underworld. If nowhere else, as it seems, history should at least find its true judge in the young and the studious. How is the youth to know what will be right for tomorrow, if the wrong remains hidden in yesterday?

If the present-day unhappy competition with the East is to be taken seriously, it isn't a greater number of mediocre people that will tip the balance, but rather a greater number of original minds. It is this self-thinking that should be prime object of all teaching, in which program the science data are never a goal, but only a means. After all data have been recounted and copied, nothing has been accomplished of significance. Nearly all of it remains shelf wisdom—and not self-improvement. In science the processes of discovery and research are the proper subject of attention, and nothing else.

In the humanities the evaluation of deeds and concepts is of import, and not the cold presentation of figures and foibles. With few exceptions the so-called historic personages, be they Caesars or Alexanders, Napoleons or Stalins, are monsters of this earth, which they drenched with the blood of its people. Where are the historians who write of the people, and the events that molded their fate for the better? And how much do those who went through our present-day schools know of the life and work and the struggle of the common man, the end of which is still afar?

I greet you,

SEX AND SAGACITY

My dear Teacher:

THE scope of education may be two-fold: first, the obtaining of knowledge; second, the acquisition of social talents.

The search for knowledge is almost instinctive and can usually be traced in the simple animal that seeks out a cave for shelter and fruit-bearing plants or weaker animals for food. It will further use its body's wisdom to find water, salty rocks, helpful herbs to ease its colic and sometimes, when tender-fleshed, an empty shell as a shield.

Man, too, is engaged in this unending search for food, shelter, spices and medicinal herbs and contemporary man's endeavors still are dedicated, in the main, to satisfying the animal's needs.

As the millennia go by, there seem to be additional pursuits which growingly preoccupy our minds, namely, the preparation of signally complicated weapons of mass-destruction, and a striking concentration on multiple forms of vulgar amusement with sexual connotation. In fact, a mere glance at our newsstands and our book stalls with their mass of gory and gaudy book jackets should convince one that never in history was so much written and painted about sexual variations and perversions as in our time. It almost seems as if sex has moved from the bedroom to the parlor and the library. It has even crept into the physician's office where, in the United States, for instance, almost 10,000 devotees of Aesculapius will no longer examine your bile, liver or lungs, but, rather—like the Babylonian magicians —your dreams.

Indeed, it was told me by good authority that during the year 1960 more books were published in the United States directly or indirectly concerned with dream analysis than with all phases of medical science put together.

To come back to the beginning, man is imbued with an almost instinctive yearning to explore his environment. His preoccupation is with food and shelter. He still devours other animals but now he usually singes the pieces of flesh he has ripped off the carcass. He still washes down his food with water or the juice of pressed fruits. However, he has discovered during his years of civilization how to intoxicate his brain while quenching his thirst. He starts off one step ahead of the animal by singeing his meat and winds up one step below the animal after mixing his drink.

While this may sound like a simplification, I

would like to remind the reader that he too spends most of his working time in the task of providing food and shelter for himself and his family. It seems the animal gets his pleasure by hunting, fishing, sunning his body, eating delicacies, and, of course, giving vent to sexual desires. Man's vocation is, by and large, these same animalistic sports. I may add that man has developed a unique talent for embellishing his statistically meager sexual activity with a whole culture of imaginary byplay, called "the novel." Originating as some sort of social confessional with very serious undertones, the novel slowly deteriorated in the Eastern world to a very efficient expression of totalitarian propaganda. In the Western world it joined the ancient literary form of the stage play as a more or less subtle frame for bawdy anecdotes. Many current American stage plays and novels are no more than cleverly contrived slumming trips into red-light districts stocked with white and black trash, sordid homelife full of rapine and brutality, or nightclub shadow-land given over to adulterous intricacies and the corruption of pre-pubescent as well as post-climacteric females.

The adulterous *Lady Chatterley's Lover, Lolita, The Fugitives,* and most of the rest seem to have the same awry fascination for the intelligentsia as do the big-busted magazine and book-covers

39

for the vulgar. The difference is purely one of degree, with the vulgar being considerably closer to normal.

Besides his considerable and world-wide accomplishments in the field of herbal medicine, pharmaceutical chemistry, and the great blessing of anesthesia, man's major efforts in science have been dedicated to the principles of speed and comfort. The telephone, the telegraph, the airplane and the automobile are typical of man's tremendous speed-up in communication; on the other hand, one cannot fail to see next to the Lilliputians of peace the evergrowing monsters threatening the very existence of man, namely, nucleonics and military aviation and astronautics. "Aero-space" is already a military term before it has become a word in the civilian dictionary.

We need the study of physics, chemistry, and mathematics with their closely associated astronomy, geology and geography. At the very mention of these subjects, however, before our eyes looms the abyss of misuse of knowledge practised by the scientists of the world in the service not only of the defenders of freedom, but also of its nemesis. Scientists have inaugurated chemical, bacterial, and atomic warfare. Assassins of freedom like Hitler, Tojo and Stalin had no difficulty in persuading their own and even foreign scientists to do the bidding of Mars. And we ourselves, living in the heartland of freedom, have to strain our resources to the utmost in defense against the foreign Golems who wield the two-edged sword of atomics and electronics by raising an army of little Golems in their schools. They will acquire the robot wisdom of facts without even being touched by the grace of humanity. To them, freedom is capitalistic fancy, a repulsive concept of opponents of the so-called proletarian dictatorship, which is actually no more and no less than the tyranny of labor demagogues over the people.

The schools' subjects, outside of theoretical and applied sciences, are actually of limited, or no use in everyday life. Their varieties are meaningless in a totalitarian system, and therefore are usually altered frequently, even monthly, to suit a specific purpose.

Historic facts are twisted beyond recognition to suit a dictator's whim or wish. In their books of reference, creators become traitors, heroes turn into hoodlums, and *schlemihls* are glorified as standard bearers. They make mockery out of religion, and a religion out of muck. Saviors and sinners, victors and vanquished, dedicated and deceivers, charlatans, knights, and partisans are scrambled in a vicious merry-go-round to create a fantastic pattern of so-called "people's culture" that fits into the palm of the crafty master.

To prevent the just from falling prey to this voracious humbug, we must teach them the true values in the humanities and warn them of the involuted traps that lie in wait. In this labyrinth the red thread leads not out of perdition but rather into its maw. The mental web of totalitarianism is as intricate as it is sticky. And youth, if not forewarned, becomes its easy victim.

Science in itself without the guidance of true humanism is like an unbridled stallion lacking reins. The quicker and craftier it is, the more dangerous.

Against the cold utilitarianism of tyranny we must pit a profound and deeply rooted system of values—if we may use such a sophisticated word, divine values. We have taken God out of the schools but we have left there the devil of indolence, of indifference.

Virtue is not inborn in man, but egotism is. The seed of goodness and compassion may remain sterile for all time if it is not brought to life and growth. It serves the tyrants in their sinister planning to let that seed be dormant and die in darkness. It is difficult indeed to reach the youth of a captive world, but for this difficult task it is essential to clarify to our own young generation the meaning of life's true values.

The great and inspired leaders of mankind spoke of the divine principle in man; man's love to fellow man and man's love to God. We have no better word to replace "God," as we have no better word for "love," to signify man's humanity to man.

42

We must teach our young to look upon every phase of history and literature, art and philosophy, religion and politics, from the point of view of the divine principle of man's inner goodness.

Without such humanity we will only raise robots of science on either side of the iron curtain. Today science is as much a threat as it is a blessing. Let the humanities tip the scale.

I greet you,

EXISTENTIALISM IN SCHOOL

My dear Teacher:

IF the world's educational systems be compared to motorized vehicles they certainly don't run on all their cylinders. The overwhelming majority of the three billion living today receive no education at all. One can certainly not euphemize the bit of reading and writing they get with the nomen education. On the other hand, this would be an impossible world if all its inhabitants, male and female alike, were imbued with the equivalent of a doctor's degree. Most of the tasks demanded of the peasants or laborers, soldiers and attendants, in the Asian and African world and many of those in the Western sphere are of a rather simple nature. If, theoretically speaking, we were all capable of handling the fine mechanics of society we would have no one for the common chores. The majority of what populates this globe has little interest—shall I say, fortunately?—in arranging so exalted a future for their offspring. They would rise so high above their parents that in their fright, the parents actually would lose them. Occasionally such metamorphosis is possible. But it is limited by the local supply and demand.

Basically there always have been two approaches to education. One is the existentialist attitude which sees in the state a kind of Platonic end in itself and will therefore compress the young mind into a form that will produce the most effective members of the state organization. In the present era of industrial and scientific competition, the existentialist state, such as the Russian, for instance, or the Chinese, will concentrate with utter disregard of all pedagogic considerations on the mass-development of a technically minded generation, hoping in this way to surpass alleged competitor-states. If such existentialist procedure be ultimately successful, that is a problem in itself.

Diametrically opposed to the above position is the essentialist and democratic attitude in which not the existence of the state, but rather the welfare or the essence of man is the final educational aim. In such a society the just are given free choice of school and profession. Here the state is merely a protector of the health, security and welfare of its citizens. Choice, as well as emphasis, is left to parents and pupils.

On the face it appears that the existentialist, directive state should carry off the winning pennant. If it wants engineers or physicists, mathematicians or chemists, it can direct the youth at its mercy into the appropriate school channels en masse, discriminatorily if so desired, and push them through with utter disregard of non-existentialist subjects or preferences of the individual. In contrast, society dedicated to essential ideas can, at most, use only methods of persuasion in its democratic tradition of suggestion and advice.

Still, history proves irrefutably that the United States, being an essentialist society par excellence without even a trace of Federal dominance of the school system, has managed to perform in undisputed pre-eminence in most fields of science and industry and at the same time maintain a standard of living topping by far the actual level of all the existentialist dictatorships.

Perhaps it is true that a state can produce, by insensitive pressure, a great number of mediocre technicians, but not an overwhelming number of professionals imbued with genius and imagination.

Many of us are critical of the American educational systems but we should be critical because we wish to deepen the essence of our own

47

community. What we have to fear is not being overcome by Red miracle workers but being handicapped or even defeated by black forces within our own walls.

I greet you,

THE STILL VOICE

My dear Teacher:

RABBI Baruch Spinoza once said, "The essential principle of religion is not doctrine but love." A variation of this proposition is found in Pestalozzi's "the basic principle of education is not teaching, it is love."

In an era like ours, in which the churches can look back upon a hundred generations of theological strife, wars and persecutions, Spinoza's principle sounds as out of place as the Swiss folk teacher's plea for humanity when Red demagogues and Western admirals plead for more and more withdrawal of teaching into the tool closets of science.

It was Philo Judaeus of Alexandria who scrutinized the schools of the Romans, which by then were dominant from one end of the Mediterranean Basin to the other. Of course, they were private and limited to Roman citizens, and among those, to the patricians. Had they been public institutions in Caesarean hands their influence could hardly have been more clear-cut in creating a race of dominant, self-perpetuating cliques, the admission price to which was birth, wealth, or ambition. But the real *conditio sine qua non* was unquestioned acceptance of Tiberian apartheid.

What we see in the wide realm of the Soviet Empire is only a magnification of Caesarean pedagogy: training in the subjects that can be used most efficiently in the obtaining of Caesarean goals, with major emphasis on military science and economic domination.

Persons outside of the party system are tolerated only insofar and inasmuch as they cooperate in the victory of Communist development; and countries outside the Communist pale are looked upon either as possible objects of propaganda and infiltration, or, if non-cooperative, as barbaric strongholds of Capitalism, to be destroyed at the proper time.

The Marxist threat to bury the capitalist world is as sincere and real as the Roman efforts to destroy Carthage or Israel. And the Russo-Chinese cutlass aristocracy was as little squeamish about rubbing out a million or two opponents of its scheme, as the Romans were about throwing a few thousand captives to the lions as a form of amusement at festivals, or chaining an army of obstreperous Asians to their galleys.

In both instances, the conquistadors of Rome and those of the Kremlin, we find educational

systems concentrating on the sciences and applied technologies to the utmost. They make sure that their students are given a sufficient amount of general information in history, geography and the languages so as to be able to spread their devious principles successfully. Such neutral games and preoccupations as music, poetry and dance are given a niche in their state structure as harmless, and perhaps helpful, decorations to intrigue strangers and to lull the people into a feeling of having at least the freedom of entertainment. No one can fail to see that even those "frills" of life in school are rigidly adjusted as part of the great machinery arranged to control every phase of the people's life.

We have said it before, and we say it again —the educated person is not a better person because of his or her knowledge, but only a more dangerous one.

The most educated nations, the Caesarean Romans, the Hitlerian Germans, or the Stalinist Russians have the most revolting deeds on their conscience, or where the conscience should be.

It is conscience that distinguishes good men from evil, and not an array of facts stored up in the brain. And it is lack of conscience that accounts for the fundamental failure of educational systems in the West as well as in the East.

Out of the 100,000 physicians of Hitler's Germany the records fail to show a single member

protesting against the horrid vivisections perpetrated on forcibly hospitalized Jews; and little more than a half dozen years ago in the Soviet Union when a group of Jewish doctors, classified as such by the indictment, were accused of poisoning statesmen, all local as well as state medical societies of the country sent telegrams the very night of the indictment demanding that those doctors be executed immediately. It is instructive to note that, the day following, numerous Leftist medical societies in the satellite countries, and even in France, hastened to fall in line with their own clamor for execution before they had even the slightest evidence presented to them.

Without wanting to put our own medical societies on the same level with totalitarian opportunists, I feel it only fair to point out that very few of our medical associations in the North, and none in the South, give the Negro physicians full membership. To go further, our scientific associations practice, with few exceptions, more or less emphatic segregation, far more than our unions or farmers' cooperatives.

In the South as well as in the North more bars are open to Negroes than churches, and more cinemas than schools.

It seems, with all the subjects on the curriculum, there is one woefully missing—the theme of human conscience. I for one agree with the ancient rabbinical adage: "If you have all the wis-

doms of all the worlds and you lack the wisdom of love, you are an *Amhaaretz,* a peasant"—which in those days meant an ignorant man.

Perhaps Pestalozzi was right, as were the ancient Talmudists, in claiming that the basic principle of education was the wisdom of love.

Nothing is easier to teach than hate; that is perhaps the reason why tyrants invariably find someone or something for their people to hate. With this hatred they unite them; with this hatred they hold them—it comes easy to man.

But the teaching of love is difficult; and it is shameful indeed that so many of the professed teachers of love, those who speak in the name of the Prince of Love, forget their own teachings when they close the church door. They call all men God's children in Moscow and Kiev, but they are subtle when it comes to overlooking anti-Semitism; they preach the Sermon on the Mount over and over again, but they practise apartheid from Capetown to Birmingham.

They may have learned the science of theology and the management of churches, homiletics and Christology, eschatology and church history, but they haven't learned the wisdom of love.

If what they have learned and what they preach is religion, the schools are well off to have been separated from it. But with the preachers and the priests walked out the good Lord; the schools are left with nothing but the class subjects, and that is not enough. We have raised generation after generation of more or less educated people, and the educated are no better than the dull—frequently worse, quite frequently so. The wisdom of love, the knowledge that goodness to fellowman is the fundamental principle of human society, is as rarely introduced into our schools as it is into our politics or our churches, regardless of creed. Man can get along with much less science than he has today. As it is, very little of it goes into the healing crafts and so much of it into machinery of destruction.

We live no better together on this globe in our time than the cavemen did a hundred thousand years ago; and we have massacred in our generation many more people than in all previous known history.

Science certainly is not the answer to our great problems—not by a missile shot. Science may bind a few wounds, but then again, it will cut many more gashes. Science may have harnessed nature—who will now harness science?

The wisdom of love must be learned from one end of this globe to the other if we are to raise generations that are to be better than we are, and our ancestors were. There are great textbooks: the Psalms of King David and the Proverbs of his son; the Blessings of Isaiah and Jeshu, of Ben Sirach and Moses; the Tao Te Ching of Laotse and the messages of the enlightened, of

Gauthama Buddha, the Vedas and the Vedantas; the philosophy of Socrates and that of Spinoza. The songs are here, but where are the voices?

Unless we find the voices, and they become attuned to these great songs, we will keep on sending into the world new and newer generations with robot heads and robot hearts.

We need God back in the schools, this time not as a messenger of a church, but speaking for Himself.

I greet you,

SCIENCE WITHOUT A FACE

My dear Teacher:

IT is commonly assumed that men who have devoted a considerable part of their time to scientific research are, *eo ipso,* better citizens and better people. Put to the test of statistical inquiry, however, there appears no solid foundation for this assumption.

For instance: while common laborers have for a long time worked side by side, black men and white, the medical associations of the whole South and the majority of those in the North refused to accept the Negro as a full member. The Negro will have extreme difficulty in joining various learned societies as a regular member, although quite a few may permit him to attend certain of the public meetings and conventions. The few exceptions rather confirm than undo this silent scholars' agreement.

It is fascinating as well as unpleasant to note that even the clergy is, in the majority, segregated as are the churches. In cases of violent "white council" tactics, from Little Rock to Birmingham, the voices of the local clergymen seem to be muted in the very heart of their churches. No trumpet of Christian love, scarcely a peep was heard protesting the pagan humiliation of a handful of black boys and girls at the hands of sneering white high-school classmates!

How could it be different? The sneer was born right in the homes of the well-educated parents, doctors, lawyers and teachers and nothing these kids learned in school was designed to relax the sneer.

Whatever these children learned in highschool, like whatever their parents had learned a generation before, was not meant to make them better people. It was intended merely to make them better earners of money and, perhaps, of prestige. As long as educational blueprints are drafted on a foundation of success instead of citizenship and humanship they will never produce more than smart professionals.

The doctor who practices in a hospital that refuses to bind a Negro's wound; the clergyman who pontificates from a pulpit that never faces a Negro; the teacher who writes on a blackboard "For Whites Only"; the physicist employed in a laboratory in which the colored man is a synonym for porter; the judge, who in a case of a nonwhite plaintiff or defendant, becomes, by a flip of his hand toward a malevolent jury, midwife to a miscarriage of justice—all those scientists, clergymen and other educated people are a devastatting argument against any contention that learning of the kind that is being dished out in the Western and Eastern world alike has brought about, or will bring about, betterment of mankind.

Some people assume that we are more civilized now than people were in the remote days of the Mongolian conquerors. Yet in no time of known history have so many people been massacred as in our generation and never with such brutality, never with so little pity and without any trace of remorse.

Titus shed bitter tears at the sight of Jerusalem before he went on leveling it; Attila the Hun could be persuaded by supplication to spare Rome; Caesar and Xerxes were prone to mercy.

But among approximately three billion people no voice could be found that would halt the garroting hands of Hitler or stem the sinister intent of the German nation to annihilate the Jewish women and children of Europe. In this last decade could a measure be devised to stay the executioner's axe wielded by Stalin and Mao?

This generation stands at the grave of almost forty million assassinated and the doom has not ceased. Our generation has cut down more children and women and other civilians than all the generations of known history put together.

Whatever science and its education has inspired, it has not strengthened the voice of humanity and not helped the weak in distress.

Science serves the wicked as readily as the well-meaning. Often we have witnessed the flight of scientists from lands of freedom like our own, England, or France to countries where vitriolic tyrants governed. Some did not flee to the dictator's lair; they prefer, rather, to remain in the security of our democracies while doing the enemy's bidding by whitewashing his crimson shield and besmirching the banner of their native country. Thus they live vicariously in the nimbus of the totalitarian overlord, sometimes encouraged by Stalin Prizes and Hitler medals, at other times repaid in ways not yet known.

We have had Nobel prize-winners behave like Casablanca barroom agents and scientists with illustrious names shame the muses all in one. Science can be less a step toward culture than an impediment to humaneness. The Nobel prize-winners were as ready to make an atom bomb for Hitler, and they almost succeeded, as they were to do later for Stalin.

Science does not make better men but rather more dangerous ones.

I greet you,

THE ART OF BEING HUMAN

My dear Teacher:

SINCE the days of Pestalozzi men have tried to set down a philosophy of modern education. Programs were designed, curricula were prepared aimed at helping develop a good human being.

No one, however, seems to have taken the trouble to define "a good human being." Is it a boy with the highest grades in math or chemistry? Is it a girl with the best paper in literature, art or history?

In our own generation we had a whole nation of the Western world, most proficient in all subjects that seemed to matter, yet they got up one autumn morning and started a berserk attack on six million unarmed men, women and children from all over Europe, putting them through the most awful forms of execution by starvation, torture and suffocation.

The rest of the world stood by, most of them making believe they did not see it, while most of those who saw gave a sigh and let the matter stand where it was. Very few did anything at all. Later, when this great planned massacre was about to be ended other powers became involved. With this the German nation, for entirely different reasons, put an end to the expiring macabre spectacle.

After the Germans were defeated they went back and re-established the same old school system which obviously had been no impediment to 70 million citizens running amok.

We have seen this process repeat itself on a smaller, perhaps, but still frightful scale in Stalin's Russia, in Mao's China, in Nasser's Egypt, leaving a trail of dungeons, concentration camps and putrid propaganda.

What is wrong with the people who do the bidding of tyrannical monsters? What makes people not only suffer the inhumanities and indignities imposed by avaricious dictators, but, I ask, *what* makes them cheerfully, even gleefully, carry out such demands?

What is wrong with the school systems of Western and Eastern world alike that encourages the raising of sycophants, of sadistic sycophants, generation after generation?

Our own country is not to be overlooked. What is wrong with our schools in the south that a black man cannot find twelve among his white peers even to indict his son's slayers, that a black woman cannot find a judge even to listen to her tale of kidnaping and torture?

I have already told you what is wrong with all those schools: They have taken God out of the schools and left the devil in them—the devil of arrogance, the devil of prejudice, the devil of greed and the devil of envy, the devil of denunciation and the devil of aggressiveness, the devil of subservience and the devil of egotism.

They have taken out of the school the God of the book of Moses, the God that is love; the God of King David, the God that is generosity; and the God of King Solomon, the God that is humility. They teach you a hundred subjects in these schools—everything except ethics, the art of being human, the art of being humane.

What good is all geography, knowing the look of people across the seven seas if you don't know your neighbor across the yard? What good is knowing history, the Caesars of Rome and the Pharaohs of the Nile, if you don't want to understand the man across the street? Or knowing distant poets, playwrights and spinners of tales if you can't hear the black man's dirge or the Jew's song right in your own time! And what good is knowing the secrets of the atom and the science of light and space, if all it brings is more and more power into the fists of demagogues? They think they are ripping at the hem of God but all they have is the devil by his tail.

All knowledge is without avail if humanity is not its guide. Those who master science are not better for it, only more dangerous, if they themselves are not mastered by conscience and responsibility.

The Germans stood at the peak of science when they turned into a horde of headhunters and the Russians stood at the peak of science while they acquiesced to annihilation.

How little God has become in our world since the schools rejected Him, and how small are all the schools bereft of His wisdom and His goodness!

I greet you,

THE RIGMAROLE OF SOCIAL SCIENCE

My dear Teacher:

THE teaching of traditional concepts as being fundamental rather than fluid—therein lies the root of pedagogic carelessness. The student is led to believe that the scope of his study is the absorption of existing principles and not their re-examination.

The diligent pupil quickly finds docility a safe buffer and, combined with subordination to scholastic regimen, the gateway to merit.

Frequently the appeal of such docile formality is enhanced by the obvious advantages inherent in traditional prejudice.

It is easier to rationalize an anthropology based on alleged superiority of the so-called Caucasian race, if one is a member of it. Very few of its "scholarly" representatives will run short of convincing arguments or ever-flexible statistics to prove their deadly point. They hardly bother to consider the fact that a short three thousand years ago the achievement score was reversed when such peoples as the Egyptians, the Israelites, the Sumerians, the Carthaginians, and colored races in the Far East were high on the scale of human culture while the Europeans were running wild with swine and bear.

It was barbaric Europe, epitomized in Rome, that leveled the temples, libraries and schools of Athens, Carthage, Alexandria and Jerusalem, and stretching a mailed fist up to Central Asia, made a desolate ending of the flowering Middle East and northern Africa.

Perhaps the thunderous rise of Africa and Asia foretells the return of the vanquished nations of antiquity to the broad paths of world progress.

Perhaps our textbooks in the humanities require complete rewriting, if possible with a touch of humaneness.

I am horrified in contemplating the ugly faces of German youth deriding a hapless Jewish minority; I am horrified in contemplating Russian crowds mocking churchgoing citizens; I am horrified contemplating the hordes of Red China watching gleefully the decapitation of millions of alleged opponents to a sinister regime; I am horrified equally by the hate in the eyes of Southern schoolboys chasing Negro students from campus or store.

It seems to me that in the face of such outrages, the rigamarole of social science in all these places is either all wrong or altogether unrealistic.

The young people in Russia, China, Germany and our own South are either presented with a cockeyed picture of anthropology or taught by implication that the text may be for the campus but life begins in the gutter, rather like the Soviet teaching of the equality of all citizens— excluding those of Jewish heritage, they being agents of the U.S.A. Akin is the attitude of those Protestant churches in the South which preach the brotherhood of man in the name of Jesus, but practice apartheid even in the cemetery.

Most of the historic, geographic and sociological data as they appear in our anthropological texts are dubious, hypothetical, or at best conjecture. A man can, and many a one does live a full and rich life unencumbered by the burden of anthropological half-intelligence. If, however, all that arbitrary categorizing, classifying and nomenclature were real, and not mere opinion, it still would cry out for most radical re-examination in view of the unsavory panorama of humiliation and persecution it has produced.

Let's not forget that our dear school-going grandparents alibied slavery, that our vociferous leftists and liberals whitewashed Stalin's bloody massacres, and that the saint-faced Nehru works hand in glove with the Arabic princes who still sell men and women like cattle in their oildoms.

The distressing part is not so much the evil doing of the dominating leaders, but rather, the indifference of the educated to tyranny and the nonchalance with which they accept sinfulness as the way of our society.

After all is said and done, the humanities should teach you, only partly, practical information for use in daily life; their main function lies in making youth into good people.

What good is a literature which excludes the black man, or a religion which keeps him outside its church, or a sociology which tolerates ghettos for Negroes, or a whole damned school that segregates pupils by pigment?

What good is a socialism that makes the Jew a pariah or the lofty thinker a state enemy?

Wherever the people submit to tyranny of evil men, the schools have utterly failed, because it is on the shoulders of the people that the dictators build their power. If the inhabitants of a state live in hatefulness and humiliating segregation, it is the school that teaches or tolerates arrogance and malevolence. Hear these young scholars sneer and rant against their black neighbors, and you will understand the insufficiency of their lesson.

Some plead for patience and gradualness. If a hundred years after Lincoln did not do it, another ten of Faubus will not.

I greet you,

EDUCATION AND THE PARTY LINE

My dear Teacher:

No dictator ever questioned the value of education. From the days of the power-drunk Caesars to the era of Russia's power-greedy labor leaders, education has been a matter of prime consideration. The Peking Caligula even wrote tender poetry and essays on morals for the benefit of the coming generations of communal serfs.

A properly educated individual will make a properly behaving party member. Of course, the discipline is carefully laid out to ensure a correct intellectual response to the political and social twists that lie before the unsuspecting on the winding road of the respective masterminds.

For many generations the fate of most of the world's people has been masterminded by cunning usurpers. These men found it imperative to sway the educated, and even more, to educate the young.

The cream of Nazism was skimmed off the universities of Germany, and the new aristocracy of the Soviet empire is forcibly drawn from the schools of higher education. Thus the educated do not become better persons, but rather more dangerous ones.

Education in itself is no remedy against evil doing or evil thinking. Acquisition of scientific facts is ethically meaningless, as the scientist will serve the devil as readily as the saint. Hitler's Germany or Stalin's Russia never had a problem of finding willing scientists for the execution of their nefarious projects or weapons. Indeed, quite a few of our own Paulings or Oppenheimers, who were squeamish about U.S. war preparedness, demonstrated astonishing naïveté in viewing Stalin's schemes. Some of the outstanding physicists of England and France betrayed their republics for the murderous Russian dictator.

As far as the other areas of education are concerned, the humanities, those are highly opinionated, and a mere glance at any historic period shows that the opinions educationally dominant in the humanities are those of the dictator, not those of social conscience.

Students in the Hitler era had as a steady educational diet the superiority of their Nordic race, although for thousands of years Germany's population was fathered mainly by Slavs and Wends; in literature they were told a fantastic story of German world importance, while in fact Germany's literature began quite late in the 18th century, except for a few ballads and folk tales. When China had its golden period of Li Po and Tu Fu, Germany did not even have a literary language of its own. Hitler's students were coddled with sweet self-praise along racial lines. Anthropology became a family album of conceited nationalistic poses. In history the Germans were made out to be the veritable chromosomes of knightsmanship and state-wisdom, while in fact they were living from one assault on their neighbors to another, be it Austria or Czechoslovakia, Poland, Denmark, Holland, Belgium, France.

Naturally, every German accomplishment in art was grossly exaggerated, and hundreds of accomplished men of Europe, even if they only had a German name or grandparent, were listed in the Nazi book of art appreciation.

A quite similar false emphasis is discernible in other dictatorships, such as Soviet Russia, where the achievements of Western discoverers and inventors are either denied or disparaged, and attributed to Russians. Not a single page in Communist history books comes even near the truth; indeed the treatment of their own people is so erratic and subject to change of opinion by the current party leader, that paragraphs, pages and chapters in reference books are regularly rewritten to please a new political master.

This morass of falsehoods running through the humanities in Soviet countries does not stop them from pursuing a sober and solid road in the fields that matter to them, namely science and technology, with emphasis on their military aspects.

A muddlehead in the social arena can evidently be made into an accurate and effective scientist.

This unpleasant fact is to be borne in mind as pressure mounts for more and better science education, lest we create, like the Soviets, efficiently operating robots without faith or conscience.

I greet you,

LANGUAGE AND SYMPATHY

My dear Teacher:

I remember as if it were yesterday your lecture on harmony, the final goal of education. Who would want to deny that the building of a harmonious personality is as good a pedagogical aim as any? You were very clear in your exposition; you didn't fail to stress that the curriculum is based on a two-pronged aim: (1) to teach matters of practical use to be applied in professional life; and (2) to teach esoteric subjects aimed at encouraging the bloom of well-rounded personality.

As far as the practical matters are concerned, I would say the teaching of mathematics, physics, chemistry and sundry biological themata is something no one will argue with in principle, only in detail. For instance, chemistry and physics are more often than not reduced to rote treatment of abstractions, having little or no effect upon either the knowledge or the mind of the student. In biology, especially in zoology and botany, an intricate nomenclature is foisted upon the uncooperative student who would flourish by much less of that medicine and much more of the field work that makes for true understanding of all processes of growth and procreation.

The study of foreign languages, which lies somewhere in between applied subjects and the esoteric ones, stands by itself in oblivion. Some foreign country, especially a hostile one, will make excessive strides in one phase of science or another—as Russia, for instance, does these days—and the school supervisors and principal rush into accelerated study of foreign languages: little of Russian, of course, but rather Italian, Spanish, French and German, as if more emphasis on these languages would be helpful toward understanding of Russian and Chinese scientific problems! It is true that there is a reluctance among most teachers as well as parents to become excited about the study of Russian, but certainly the intensified study of Continental languages will be another colossal waste of the students' time.

I would like to see one student who after four years of formal education in French or Italian, German or Spanish, can appreciate fully the beauty of the respective native literature as he or she could in one of the magnificent available translations penned by highly specialized writers.

In practically all cases the student is so busy with the absorption of a vocabulary and grammar, that he rarely, if ever, acquires the fine aesthetic powers of literary appreciation in that particular tongue. I say again and again, instead of spending thousands of school hours in old-fashioned analysis of foreign languages, let the literature of that foreign country be studied in its many classic translations. Then the student will, after four years or five, be able to justly say, "I have a good knowledge of the literature of France or Germany," instead of, as today, acquiring a lifelong disdain for the language or, perhaps, succeeding in his effort, on a vacation trip to Europe, to order his dinner in the native tongue or read one of the miserable little Italian librettos.

In the city of Dallas, Texas, and its environs, covering a territory of a few thousand square miles, over 200,000 pupils have studied Latin, Greek, Spanish, French, Italian and German. There isn't a single bookstore in that whole area which stocks adult books in any of these languages. That means, if I am correct, that none of these 200,000 persons ever had a desire after leaving high school or college to continue reading literature in the languages they were oppressed with anywhere from two to six years.

The public libraries in the vicinity bear this out even more clearly, since the few borrowers of the few available foreign language literary works were almost exclusively—except for students, of course—people with whom the language in question had been mother tongue.

The study of foreign languages should be left to those who wish to make a profession or an avocation of it, in the same manner as the study of the piano, or draftsmanship. There is no need to burden a million students with the drudgery of multiple language synonyms if only one in 10,000 is likely to wish to continue professionally the pursuit of that particular language. Let this wasted time be used to give the class a much needed knowledge of foreign literature and foreign people. I have found that by and large the students of Spanish know little of the many great works of Spanish literature, except the watered-down excerpts they came across in the language readers, frequently with little numbers dotting the sides to facilitate day by day identification of the assigned passage. No matter how many pieces you cut out of Goethe's *Faust*, paragraph by paragraph, no matter how smartly teacher identified verb, noun and odd vocabulary, this will never take the place of reading the book in one continuous sweep in a fine translation.

In many cases the foreign pieces used in school work are partly rewritten by "simplification" of sentence structure and "replacement" of some of the vocabulary. To appreciate the really fine points of literature, the particular grace and beauty of a writer or the subtlety of his idiomatic expression, it takes many, many years of reading in the language without "instant-interpretations" by footnotes, teachers' explanations and other references.

There are literary specialists in the field who have spent a lifetime rendering these foreign words into our tongue, and these translators are capable of unraveling the intrinsic beauty of the foreign masterpieces in all their grandeur.

The only thing the students in our language classes seem to acquire is a deep chagrin at their incapacity, or else a thoroughgoing indifference to what is offered to them as foreign literature.

I wish you would make an inquiry among your own students who went to class with you ten, twenty or thirty years ago, and ask them what was the last book they read in Greek or in Latin, in German or Italian.

I would say that this dedication to purposeless language study is harmless, were it not for the fact that so much good could be done with the time thus thrown away. And in the process of harmonizing personality, I doubt if the individual student's rapidly dwindling French or German vocabulary adds to his stature.

Now let's think for a while about the esoteric school subjects, such as the social sciences, history, ethics, anthropology and other cultural affairs.

To what extent have our schools succeeded in raising and upholding the cultural level of the youth? When I use the term "our schools" I don't mean just the schools of America or the schools of today. I mean, rather, the schools of the Western world and the Eastern world, going back thousands of years, since the changes that have afflicted them are so few and far between that it is hardly worthwhile to make a distinction between then and now. It is true, mathematics, physics and chemistry have changed considerably from the days of antiquity. But when we consider the cultural subjects, in what way did they affect the youth? What impact did our teachings have upon the people, young and old? How did they sway them, if at all?

Let's take the Romans. They were in the habit (and the habit persisted for many hundred years) of collecting hundreds of captives, criminals, and minor offenders against official regulations, and, on certain festival occasions, making them suffer capital punishment at the hands of man and wild beast alike. These circuses were not put on merely for the pleasure of the masses, but were also conceived as a penal deterrent for the benefit of all citizens and slaves alike who lived in the grace of Pax Romana. I don't think that these circuses outdid in cruelty the gassing of millions of Jewish women and children at the hands of brown-shirted gladiators a decade or two ago.

I further doubt that the axing of dissidents in

the market places of Mao Tse-tung's China was less revolting than Rome's crimson holidays. And it should be noted that, numerically, the victims of Caesar in almost a thousand years didn't come near the obscene totals of those executed by Hitler, Stalin and Mao.

The amazing thing is that neither the students of ancient Rome nor those of contemporary Germany, and certainly not the scholars of Russia and China, seem to have been inspired in the slightest to protest against the macabre slaughter of people.

Must not one ask oneself and others the question: what type of cultural education have we that such monstrosities can occur, and our young (to say nothing of those who have graduated from these schools) do not bat an eyelash?

What kind of history are these young scholars taught? What kind of ethics? What kind of social science?

Perhaps they spend too much time learning what bust of what corrupt Senator was made by what sculptor at what time. Or what portrait of what bloody Duke or what churchman was painted by what painter and when. Or what Arch of Triumph was erected by what Caesar to honor what general or what murderous conquest of neighboring peoples.

The history of Rome is the history of Mediterranean banditry for a thousand years, leaving in

ashes Carthage and Corinth, Athens and Jerusalem, Alexandria and all the thousand towns and
cities of Greek and Hebrew civilization.

And what kind of history do they learn of the
European continent, except the nightmarish in-
trigues, dungeonings and assassinations in the
courts and palaces of that bloody tailend of Eu-
rasia? The hacking and spearing of the peasant
militias of the various lords and overlords is all
that is commemorated by battle names, battle
places, and battle dates.

Oversized biographies of gilded highwaymen
are offered to our children as "history." It is no
wonder, with such outrages and ugly banalities
for "lessons in history," that the young accept the
cruelties of their own times as a matter of course.

When your grandfather or mine was a boy,
even in America people were auctioned off on
the same platform with grain and cattle. And our
youth of the South went to school and passed by
the shouting auctioneers haggling away human
flesh, and they said nothing. This is the most vicious crime of them all, the crime of omission, of
omitting to do something when faced with evil.

Where was the outcry against the peddling of
human flesh? It wasn't there. What *was* there
was the yell for the bloodhounds, with the whole
town forming a posse to hunt down the poor
black devil who ran away.

Where is the outcry of the youth of South

Africa in our own days against the beating down of fellowmen just because they want to be free or at least respected as men? The children of South Africa go to the same schools we do; they go to similar universities and colleges, and so did their parents. What is wrong that they are so silent?

What is wrong with education in our own South, in Red China, in the whole Soviet Empire, in South Africa, in the Arabic countries, where there are still over two million slaves in actual physical bondage? Why does youth remain silent, and by its silence, approve? Have they not learned right from wrong? Good from evil?

Of what value are all the bits of disjointed intelligence, bits of false history, bits of foreign languages, bits of art information, bits of falsified anthropology, pasted together with mathematics, physics, chemistry and biology? What kind of horrible harmony do they make, youthful personalities who seem to have snatched up a bit of everything except love for fellowman?

I greet you,

SHRINKING THE PAST

My dear Teacher:

ALL education is purposeful, although I must admit that frequently its teleology escapes me. Interferences with the true purpose of education are manifold. Some are purely traditional, like the study of the Greek language in Continental schools, or their intensive preoccupation with Greek mythology and Caesarean piratic wars. Large textbooks covering these and similar branches of historicity have had an overbearing existence in the Western world for millennia, taking up cuckoo's space in the nest of our children's capacity.

What possible advantages could accrue to youth from the sordid data of the marauding Roman *soldatesca* or the fanciful, obscene Olympic jealousies, with Father Zeus outdoing Casanova in fornication and the heavenly mothers of that disreputable hill enjoying celestial romance with swans, bulls, goats and mere peasantry.

In addition to this traditional ballast slowing

down the wheels of essential intelligence, the roads ahead are blocked by impediments of local character, details of the alleged deeds and veiled misdeeds of home-grown ancestry, be such of blue blood (I personally think yellow would be the appropriate color) or the Communist variety, most significantly identified with the color red.

In this case, of course, history is as heavily doctored as the current Ministry of Education feels necessary. Catherine the Great is no longer described as a benevolent motherly ruler instead of the raving nymphomaniac she was, but on the other hand, I have seen textbooks of quite recent Russia in which the bloodshot monster, Stalin, was pictured smiling benignly, just one step behind Lenin and two steps behind the Creator. I could never see the Czar as Father Russia, nor can I appreciate Stalin as the Grandpa.

The local histories of the People's Republics are forever changing, and the man who big brother learned was a savant and gentleman, the younger son discovers in his new schoolbook to be a savage and a lecher. The same, of course, holds good for other so-called labor governments or military governments. I remember when Mrs. Peron had her picture facing the Holy Mother. Letting the poor deluded woman rest, I would say only that her husband is marked down in the current schools of Argentina as a despoiler of children.

It is indeed amazing how local histories in some countries manage to blow up unimportant events little like balloons and, on the other hand, to shrink a Zeppelin to football size.

Present-day German schoolbooks, for instance, enlarge upon the short-lived Democratic era between 1918 and 1933 as if it were the total chronicle of the Teutonic twentieth century, while somehow the years of the Hitler dragon between 1933 and 1945 evaporate into invisibility, like Siegfried under the magic cap.

Getting closer to home, we are accustomed to refer to the mid-Victorian era as a charming, naïve time of gentility, tact, sobriety and "tut-tut." Like hell it was! The whole nineteenth century of England was blood and powder and cold steel. The plains of Asia and Africa are covered with the crimson memories of colonial massacres—French, British, Dutch and others. Some of these massacres are not yet over. Others, true enough, ceased when better men became of influence, men who threw the old textbooks away and began to think on their own. The acts of liberation were sponsored less by the men with the old school tie than by those who came from the docks and the factories.

History can become a second nature, and one can live a long time ignoring the first.

A third obstacle to acquiring correct discipline is man's pride and arrogance. Parliamentarians are in the habit of referring to it as "patriotism," when they are really not bent upon doing justice to their own Pater but, rather, injustice to the neighbors. This narcissism is exemplified in such exclamations as "We Nordics," "We Whites," "We of the Grand Nation," "We of the People's Republic," "We of the Holy Faith." All this is no more than braggadocio. It is no better than if one were to say: "We Joneses are the smartest people in town; we are the most cultured, the most scientific—in fact, we are the best." So-called patriotism is merely family bragging on a grand scale, which camouflages its inherent vulgarity by bigness. One feels perfectly all right in saying "We Germans" or "We Russians," while the same person would feel awkward saying "We Hitlers," "We Khrushchevs."

In our own country we are threatened less by an international than a *group* arrogance. While our group arrogance is intensified only in a limited sector of the country, it is dangerous because of its chronic character. It doesn't call out, like other patriotisms, for war, blood or extermination, but insidiously, almost silently, sabotages the minds of the people of our South. The churches preach equality of all of god's children, but they are the first to refuse baptism to a Negro babe.

The laws operate under a Constitution that guarantees all citizens freedom in the pursuit of their happiness, but they will more often than not fail to recognize a crime committed against a black man by a member of the sallow race which euphemistically refers to itself as white. And the schools—yes indeed, the schools—they teach democracy, but strictly beyond our own county. They teach biology, but somehow, on every page of text by gentleman's agreement there is a silent exclusion clause, and it is that segregative aside which dominates their pedagogy, not the verity of the official sciences.

In our own blessed South, Christ stops at the doorstep, the law protects the criminal and not the victim, and the school teaches a unity it doesn't believe in and practices a separation which it doesn't teach.

It seems that a good part of the world lives within a false and pretentious maze which shuts out the great truths beyond. Isn't it time we left this facade-trap and started living life all over again from real people to real people instead of from graven image to graven image?

I greet you,

ART AND THE GIFT OF GAB

My dear Teacher:

Two-dimensional art has been rapidly coming to the foreground. What was once a rare pre-occupation of a few gifted or dedicated persons has spread (mainly in this country) wider and wider, and I must say, thinner and thinner. Children of six are cautiously kept away from the rigors of the alphabet, yet turned over with abandon to a big pad and a mess of fingerpaint. The alphabet may stultify their personality, but the happy jests of colorful smears will develop it! From kindergarten to the graduate school, art has become a major topic.

In earlier centuries painting (and when I speak here of art I am referring to that particular form) was taught by painters who not only showed craftsmanship but also a fair understanding of the mechanics and history of art products.

The average teacher of today, or should I say "teacher of art appreciation," is endowed with little, if any, knowledge of canvas or palette and is in the habit of dealing with what he condescendingly calls "traditional art" in an almost patronizing manner.

The art teacher could not paint a barn door, be it subject or object, but can he talk, especially where there is no object! Non-objective art, which is the accepted designation for sundry dabs, dots and demi-dots daubed on a long-suffering canvas, seems, especially, to open these streaming sluices of art appreciation. The heroic sculptures of ancient Greece leave these tutors speechless, as do the Dutch masterpieces or Persia's tapestry, but a speckled canvas by Miro will call forth a luxurious stream of comments. When I am faced with the written or spoken art criticism by the connoisseurs of the Abstracts, I am truly amazed: Is it humanly possible to say so much about so little?

A green zigzag on a red blob—framed, of course, in expensive wood—may send them into a virtual fit, sputtering an endless array of sheer adjectives. Of course, no two of them will ever meet in consensus. But that matters as little to them as it does to a brace of astrologers who offer different horoscopes to the very same person.

Off-hand I would say that from such tutors one can learn little about painting but quite a lot about talking.

Indeed, there is very little painting in our art classes today, but a great amount of talking. I have watched students facing a blank canvas with nothing on it but two curlicues and a blotch and talk about it for ten minutes straight. (I suppose one was later valedictorian of the class and the other runner-up.) The average art teacher of today is not only glaringly ill-equipped to teach a craft he or she does not master, but ideologically so misdirected that they are capable of squelching a young talent rather than developing it. With talentless sophistication they will nip a budding talent and cut it back into a bunch of meaningless strokes and equal dashes.

What is the cause of this deviation into the sterile and pretentious? There may be many answers to this question. An obvious one is the rise of photography. Until the end of the last century every community had its painters. The portraitist and the landscape artist were called in by the rich family or poor parish, to perpetuate their faces and decorate their churches and homes. Rembrandt and Michelangelo, Goya and El Greco, and the whole array of other brilliant masters of their craft made their living mainly by painting the faces of saints and clerics, burghers and aristocrats. Some of them, like Brueghel, would paint comical peasantry for the amusement of the palace-dwellers. Others would paint battle scenes or coronations.

With the end of the nineteenth century and the beginning of the twentieth all this began to seem rather superfluous in the face of magnificent photography, brush-colored or chemically-colored. Who would want to paint the coronation of the Queen of England and who would want to own such a painting? President Roosevelt, be it Theodore or Franklin D., will be remembered by his best photograph, not by a painted portrait, and can anyone imagine anything more ridiculous than Comrade Khrushchev painted on a horse?

As for landscape, a million films and a billion photographs have almost removed it from the realm of possible subjects. We are then left with the saints. Well, the churchmen of the recent past seem to have been iconoclasts certainly as far as new works are concerned.

Here we have the dilemma of the modern painter. True, he can go surrealistic and concoct fantastic dream arrangements; he can go impressionistic or expressionistic and offer blurred or unfinished similes of nature. But there is yet another way, a refuge for his desperate brush: escape into the nothingness of no subject and no object, where the camera cannot follow him with its effortless insatiable eye.

Thus we have the artist finding himself in a new world without things and without forms; here he can paint to his heart's content.

The break came first, perhaps, with the Russian portraitist Kandinsky. What followed Kandinsky's abstraction was more and more of it with less and less to it. Where Kandinsky wandered off from his great talent, many followed who had nothing to start with. It became so unpopular to keep one's eye on the object in this country that the remaining traditional painters found themselves struggling for recognition and to sell their works. The public was swayed into accepting old masters as precursors and prophets of what they euphemistically called modern art. They expected contemporaries to walk the Kandinsky line, or else walk the plank into oblivion.

Non-objectivism became dominant. Pieces of old iron nailed to a clothes-rack became sculpture. A set of Chinese cut-outs hanging on sticks and strings from the transom of a Peking shop became a mobile. An old piece of sackcloth nailed by Mr. Picasso with oversized hooks to a 6 x 4 frame went for a better price than any genuine American art work ever did. Designs grandmother made, plastered on a canvas by clumsy fingers, were stuck next to classics in what was once a museum.

Museums were once homes created for artistic perpetuations of the eternal values of great subjects meriting this nomen. Today some of the museums of modern art are no more than hotels for the latest concoctions of men of no, or ill, repute. Pretense and modish artifice hang where paintings should. Recently a Canadian artist packed in error his brush board, on which he cleaned his implements, instead of a painted wood panel. When, discovering his mistake, he frantically wrote to the museum, he was advised that the brush board had won the first prize in abstract art before an illustrious committee of judges. A second Jackson Pollock, no doubt, unaware of his hidden talents.

A new class of art buyers has risen, having with the old Maecenases only one thing in common: the desire to own what is "the best" and the most expensive. The press announced on its front pages recently that Picasso sold two broomsticks and a kitchen chair mounted on second-hand lumber for a quarter of a million dollars by calling it "Eternity." Naturally, an oil Maecenas bought it, for the same reason another of his ilk bought a two-nosed woman to hang over the mantelpiece. It seems that in our days artistic infamy or charlatanry is the only aesthetic form with market value.

It is profoundly regrettable that our schools, as if by command, perpetuate this folly or felony of art and mold a generation blind to beauty and deaf to harmony.

Classroom studies in art-appreciation of the past have, in a way, an advantage to work in cultural history. Paintings and sculpture as well were intimately connected with the history of their respective periods. The man, the background, even the dress and the armor bore the stamp of their milieu.

With the advent of Cubism and non-objectivism all that recedes into the mere nothingness of color and splash. You may talk for hours about the alleged aesthetic effect of two thin lines against a bold one, or the interior beauty of a Picassoesque female with one breast where nature placed it and the other one close to the small of her back. However, such disjointed relocation will develop neither knowledge nor a science of beauty, but rather a cunning technique of baseless conversationalism. I once heard an art teacher dispose of a good half hour rambling about some figurations on a piece of linoleum. If non-objective art is anything at all it perhaps could take its place as a quality of design. Such linoleum art is as old as the proverbial hills: it is to be found among many primitive peoples such as Balkan peasantry or even on our ancestral quilts.

Incidentally, the yen for the primitive as a subject to imitate is a remarkable characteristic of the so-called modernists. They seem to feel akin to children's art and the handcraft of the primitive. They make masks, ceramics and, shall we say, "designs" very close to those of the eight-year-old and the medicine man from Timbuktu. What a weird combination!

Many argue that non-objective art, semi-abstract art, Cubist art, and plain schizophrenic doodling, such as that of Paul Klee, over-pasting newspaper clippings, welding together pieces of old iron, nails, hinges, hooks and horseshoes on top of a stove pipe, that all this addled creation is truly representative of the new era of modern man. The bearded loafers, the sloppy girls, and that startling mob of wealthy middle-aged women whose fondness for the non-objective troop runs parallel to the menopause, this whole motley crowd of frustrated pseudo-artists and their all too intimate followers like to refer to what they abort as "modern art."

If one raises an eyebrow to what they present, skepticism is immediately countered by the snide insinuation that the viewer lacks comprehension of this new Thing. They remark belligerently that all great innovators of all times were discounted by the mature of their respective eras, and they point with cool nerve, although little reason, to Rembrandt, Beethoven and even Einstein. Their references usually reveal more arrogance than knowledge of cultural history.

If the rebel minority is always supposed to be right, then I must say that the voice of the critics of this aesthetic blasphemy will win out, because in this country, at least, they are in dire minority. In the schools, certainly, the men with the quick brush have won out against the working artist. The piddlers of paint, such as Jackson Pollock; the finger smearers and the dribblers; those who draw with their toes on a canvas floor; those who make with the chalk on glass in seven uneven strokes; those who doodle a mess of circles, convex and concave; those who splatter blotches on a screen or draw spools and rings and stars in blue or green; those who collate cutouts from catalogues and magazines; those who stick scrap metal together in a wild dance with a welding torch; those who chip out a hole in a rock; those who hang ringlets on plastic plates, on sticks, strings and wires—none of it is new. Most, if not all, has been done in the past by boys from six to ten having fun in the backyard or in father's workshop.

When we were kids in a little village in Rumania one of the big boys swiped a blow-torch, and we sweated together everything in metal we could lay our hands on, making what we called a "monster." In all fairness to the boys, I must say it looked better than what I have seen thus far along this line in our oil dealers' museums. Whoever has entered a Chinese market in Shanghai, Hong Kong or Peking may still remember the mobiles that hung over the shop gate. They drew attention, and some even rang little bells.

As far as the abstract canvases are concerned, those with the three smears or the two, those sprinkled and those stroked, they have existed from time immemorial, brushed by children and brushed by those mentally afflicted. It is not surprising that we have by now more than a score of serious works by psychiatrists comparing Cubistic and non-objective paintings with the work produced by the inmates of various institutions.

I never condemn the impotent in art or literature for trying to assert themselves; this is only natural. But in the case of contemporary art, we have reached a stage where pretense is repressing talent and where sterility scorns fecundity as "behind the times." And our schools play midwife to this unnatural phenomenon.

Never has art endured a tougher century than this, where in the West, under the hammer-blows of photography, its artisans were driven into the sterile retreats of Cubism and Abstractionism, while in the East the artists became civil servants of uncivil tyrants.

*　　*　　*

For the teacher the abstract artists present many difficult problems which, however, they seem to have taken in their strides. As the spot artists avoid subjects, there can, of course, be no identification of objects, discussion of their history, their expression, and so on. One can say about one painting of Miro what can be said about the second, third and last. This kind of art-appreciation talk, superlatives, or even negatives, applied to a patch of color on a canvas, can of course be duplicated facing another canvas by the same or another artist. What can you say about one set of half a dozen smears or dots offered as a painting that you can't say about another? In fact, what is there to say at all where there is no object, except "Ah!" or "Eh!" or "Oh!"?

Of course, those with a gift for gab will talk about the naked emperor's new clothes, if you will only let them. The gabby need no encouragement, and those who think will wonder in silence.

I greet you,

THE AUXILIARIES OF MARXISM

My dear Teacher:

LOOKING back at our school curriculum, I was amazed to discover how many faculties of information one can do without and still live a good life, prosper, be respected, embrace a community and finally retire with the feeling of having shared in a fruitful and full existence.

I made it my business to compare various curricula of various countries of our time, and much to my surprise, the differences were frequently deeper than the agreements. Living in a metropolitan center it was easy for me to meet with representatives of the various systems of educational organization face to face, and to examine thoroughly their scholastic development.

Under the impact of the post-Renaissance humanistic attitude towards knowledge, I myself was deeply convinced of humanistic profundity, and felt that a person without rooted intelligence in Latin, Greek, Hebrew, and their respective antiquities would turn out to be a poor specimen of modern man.

I came across, in later years, alert and sober citizens from the interior of China, India and other lands where the awareness of my humanistic background was as developed, say, as the general American comprehension of Sanskrit, Urdu, or Mong-tai.

I lived for years under the impression that Latin was an essential tongue, especially for physicians, until I came across quite a few outstanding physicians who never had been students of Latin and still were excellent anatomists or physiologists, as well as surgeons and practitioners. And a few simple queries among physicians proved beyond doubt that their Latin acumen was about the lowest among the professions. They could just as readily remember the abstruse Greco-Latin combinations of *termini technici* without knowing a paragraph of Caesar's *De Bello Gallico* or Horace's odes to his munificent benefactor. And as far as the horrid linguistic concoctions of the contemporary pharmacopeia are concerned, a taste for good Latin or Greek should be an impediment rather than an assist.

It is as little necessary to know Greek and Latin in order to become a physician as it is to know German as a basic step in the mastery of science. These are some of the typical school superstitions which have been carried over from generation to generation, contributing at best only to a colossal waste of time and energy.

It is astonishing indeed how many subjects which are deemed essential in one system of education are completely ignored in another where different subjects dominate. One is almost reminded of the medieval Knights' Schools within the walls of some of Central Europe's larger castles, where the emphasis lay on good manners, good swordsmanship, good horsemanship, good conversation, with a sparse sprinkling of theology and song.

In the schools of present-day China, for instance, the children on the elementary as well as high school level are relentlessly subjected to shrewdly planned misinformation on history and other social sciences, combined with rigorous tutoring on the infallible verities of their dictatorial taskmasters. Still, these young people grow up acquiring, in addition to sets of monstrous opinions in the humanities, a fairly sound comprehension of such subjects as mathematics, physics, chemistry and biology.

To a lesser or major degree this situation exists within the whole framework of the Soviet Empire. To sum up, the population of half of this globe is subjected deliberately to unceasing misinformation on such subjects as history, anthropology, law, philosophy, religion, literature, art, and sociology. These can be called "opinionated" faculties of knowledge, since they differ according to the authority consulted and are frequently presented in diametrically opposite forms merely because of different opinions.

In the Soviet Empire dialectical materialism as promulgated by Karl Marx is established as a sacrosanct fundamental. Consequently, all other theories of economics, sociology and philosophy are automatically derided, excluded or ignored.

In history the dominant Soviet desire is to show all events of the past as logical steps towards a final conquest of all society by Communism, and therefore all historical phenomena of the past are explained in the light, or rather, darkness, of this preconceived notion. Even the field of biology was placed under the directives of a rigid type of Darwinism, as clearly illustrated in the infamous Lysenko case. Similarly, in the teaching of psychology unalterable Pavlovism must prevail. Art is regarded as an auxiliary means of illustrating the social struggle along the Communist road to victory, and like literature, is subjected to unending censorship as well as prodding and threatening by the Soviet authorities. It is self-evident that all Russian art and literature, as well as foreign art and literature, are judged purely by their influence upon the class struggle.

As a result, leading philosophers such as Spinoza, Kant, or Bergson are brushed aside, while none but obedient Marxist penmen are elevated to Red immortality. In psychology, men like Freud, Adler, Jung, and James are referred to as lackeys of the capitalist class. And, of course, the great religious leaders from Moses—especially, Moses—to Wesley and the theologians of our time are held up to belated mockery.

Still, within this jungle of abysmal misinformation in the humanities inside the Soviet Empire (and overflowing into some neighboring countries —be their governments gullible or cunning) the subjects of abstract as well as applied science are taught in a manner not much different from ours and by methods which suit the sinister purposes of the Soviet overlords. Why such methods of cold, utilitarian competitivism should continue to be upheld by our schools is something to ponder.

I greet you,